I0042587

THE STATE OF
FOOD INSECURITY
IN HARARE, ZIMBABWE

GODFREY TAWODZERA, LAZARUS ZANAMWE
AND JONATHAN CRUSH

SERIES EDITOR: PROF. JONATHAN CRUSH

ACKNOWLEDGEMENTS

The financial support of the Canadian Government through the CIDA UPCD Tier 1 Program is acknowledged. The editorial assistance of Cassandra Eberhardt, Maria Salamone and Bronwen Müller is also acknowledged.

Cover Photograph: Desmond Zvidzai Kwande, Africa Media Online

Published by African Food Security Urban Network (AFSUN)

© AFSUN 2012

ISBN 978-1-920597-00-9

First published 2012

Production by Bronwen Müller, Cape Town

AUTHORS

Godfrey Tawodzera is the AFSUN Post-Doctoral Fellow in the African Centre for Cities, University of Cape Town.

Lazarus Zanamwe is in the Department of Geography at the University of Zimbabwe.

Jonathan Crush is Co-Director of AFSUN and Honorary Professor at the University of Cape Town.

Previous Publications in the AFSUN Series

No 1   *The Invisible Crisis: Urban Food Security in Southern Africa*

No 2   *The State of Urban Food Insecurity in Southern Africa*

No 3   *Pathways to Insecurity: Food Supply and Access in Southern African Cities*

No 4   *Urban Food Production and Household Food Security in Southern African Cities*

No 5   *The HIV and Urban Food Security Nexus*

No 6   *Urban Food Insecurity and the Advent of Food Banking in Southern Africa*

No 7   *Rapid Urbanization and the Nutrition Transition in Southern Africa*

No 8   *Climate Change and Food Security in Southern African Cities*

No 9   *Migration, Development and Urban Food Security*

No 10 *Gender and Urban Food Insecurity*

No 11 *The State of Urban Food Insecurity in Cape Town*

No 12 *The State of Food Insecurity in Johannesburg*

CONTENTS

TABLES

FIGURES

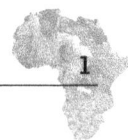

1. INTRODUCTION

Harare is the largest city and capital of Zimbabwe. At independence in 1980, the population of the city was under half a million but it grew rapidly during the 1980s primarily as a result of large-scale rural-urban migration.[1] Between 1982 and 1992 the population doubled from 565,011 to 1,189,103 (an annual growth rate of 5.9%). In the 1990s, however, the growth rate slowed to 2.1% per annum under the combined impact of structural adjustment, rising unemployment, serious housing shortages, out-migration and the HIV and AIDS epidemic.[2] Between 1992 and 2002, the population of Harare increased by only 250,000 reaching a total of 1,444,534 at the end of the period. As the country slid into economic and political chaos after 2000, the city continued to experience slow and halting growth. The current population is estimated to be 1.8 to 2 million.

The residents of Harare have lived under extraordinarily trying circumstances for the last decade. In addition to an increasingly volatile political climate, they have had to endure the virtual collapse of the national economy, record unemployment, increasing poverty and rampant inflation.[3] In 2005, the government launched a nationwide assault on informality which had a major negative impact on the urban poor of Harare who lost their homes or livelihoods or both.[4] The country's economic collapse decimated the livelihoods and savings of most households in the country and increased their vulnerability to ill-health and food insecurity. Urban households were particularly vulnerable to food insecurity because of their heavy dependence on food purchases. Most of the food in Zimbabwe's urban markets is imported, rendering the urban population more susceptible to external food shocks and rising food prices.[5]

The rural areas of Zimbabwe are usually seen as the epicentre of poverty, hunger and malnutrition.[6] However, unlike most other countries within SADC – where food insecurity is viewed almost exclusively as a rural problem – Harare has a substantial history of research on the urban dimensions of food security. In the 1990s, for example, research focussed on the functioning of the city's food system and the food security and livelihood strategies of the urban poor.[7] The dramatic growth of urban agriculture in the city and the often negative response of the city authorities were also documented in considerable detail.[8] Harare's rich tradition of research on urban poverty and food insecurity has recently shown signs of a revival.[9]

Beginning in 2003, there have also been various attempts to monitor the urban food security situation in Zimbabwe through household surveys. These surveys, conducted at regular intervals, promise to provide a

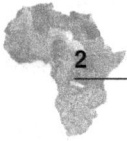

longitudinal perspective on urban food insecurity that is completely missing in other countries and cities in Africa. In theory, they should also show how food insecurity intensified in Harare as the country's political and economic crisis deepened. In practice, the changes in methodology from survey to survey make it difficult to track trends. There are also grounds for questioning the definition and measurement of food insecurity used in these surveys. For example, they seem to underestimate the extent of food insecurity and even suggest that there was a considerable improvement in urban food insecurity between 2003 and 2006. They also seem to suggest that food insecurity has never been a particularly serious problem for the majority of poor urban households in Harare.

This paper begins with an assessment of these household surveys of urban food security conducted between 2003 and 2009. It then describes an alternative methodology for measuring urban food security. This methodology was developed and used by AFSUN in a baseline household food security survey in Harare in late 2008 as part of a larger eleven-city study of Southern Africa.[10] The timing of the Harare research is important because it occurred at a time when the country's economic and political crisis was at its worst. Formal sector unemployment was over 80%, inflation was running at almost 100% per day and the country was still reeling from the effects of the highly contested election of June 2008. This study therefore provides considerable insights into the food security levels and strategies of households at the peak of the crisis. It does not purport to represent the present-day food security situation in Harare. However, it does also provide reliable baseline information from which the current situation could be assessed in order to see whether and how the food security of Harare has improved since 2008. The paper concludes by recommending that the AFSUN methodology be adopted to monitor current and future levels of food insecurity in Harare.

2. Monitoring Urban Food Insecurity

In 2001, FEWSNET and the Consumer Council of Zimbabwe (CCZ) conducted a pilot urban vulnerability assessment in Harare.[11] They interviewed 115 households throughout the city. The study used a Food Poverty Line (FPL) of Z$2,650 per month for a family of four and found that 10-20% of households were below the line, up from 7% in 1996.[12] The poorest income group (earning Z$4,000 a month or less) had an average expenditure of Z$2,700 of which Z$1,000 was spent on food. The survey included some qualitative commentary on the urban diet: "There is little variation in the diet of the poorest households. They often have two meals per day – a breakfast (composed of maize meal porridge or tea with sweet potatoes) late in the morning followed by a proper meal of *sadza* usually with vegetables in the evening. Most of their calories come from maize grain. Over 90% of calories are from maize." The findings were suggestive but the sample size was too small and the sampling methodology insufficiently randomized to provide anything other than an impressionistic picture.

The first national urban food security survey in Zimbabwe was conducted in 2003 by the SADC FANR Vulnerability Assessment Committee and the Zimbabwe Vulnerability Assessment Committee.[13] The Report accurately noted that "previous attempts to understand and monitor urban poverty and food insecurity have been fragmented and have not fully explained poverty and livelihood vulnerabilities in the urban areas."[14] The authors of the report surveyed 5,123 households in randomly selected urban sites nationwide, including 1,609 (or 31% of the total) in Harare. To measure levels of food security, the survey calculated the household caloric intake of all foods available to the family in the month of September 2003 (including purchases, urban agriculture, rural-urban transfers, gifts and food aid). The caloric intake for each household was then compared with an ideal caloric intake value. Households with a negative score were considered food insecure and those with a positive score were considered food secure. By this measure, 66% of Zimbabwe's urban population was judged to be food insecure and 37% of those households survived on less than 50% of their caloric requirements. In Harare, 63% of urban households were food insecure. The report also covered a number of related issues at the national level including variations in food security by type of household, the relative importance of different food sources and the responses of households to food adversity. However, no city specific data on Harare was provided.

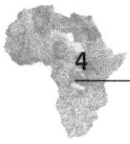

In 2006, the Zimbabwe National Vulnerability Assessment Committee conducted a second urban survey.[15] However, their methodology differed in important ways from the 2003 survey, making comparative analysis impossible. In Harare, 604 households were surveyed in high density and peri-urban areas of the city. In order to distinguish food secure from food insecure households, the report used three indicators rather than the single indicator of the 2003 study: (a) caloric intake; (b) the Food Poverty Line; and (c) a measure of dietary diversity. A food insecure household was one which failed to meet a minimum value on all three indicators (or on (a) and (b) or on (b) and (c)). Using these measures, only 24% of urban households nationally were deemed food insecure (a dramatic drop from the 66% of the 2003 study). In Harare, only 20% of households were classified as food insecure (a fall from 63%). The idea that food insecurity declined in urban Zimbabwe between 2003 and 2006 seems far-fetched given what we know about the state of the country's economy and food supply in these years. Between the two surveys, for example, the livelihoods of many low-income urban residents had been destroyed by Operation Murambatsvina. In addition, the inflation rate had increased from 599% in 2003 to 1,281% in 2006.

In January 2009, the Zimbabwe Vulnerability Assessment Committee (ZimVAC) conducted another national urban survey.[16] The sampling methodology was similar to that used in 2006, again focusing only on high-density and peri-urban areas. A total of 2,677 households were interviewed including 360 households in Harare. Using the same food security indicators, the survey found that 33% of households in high-density and peri-urban areas were food insecure (up from 24% in 2006). In Harare, the proportion increased from 20% to 31%. The report also included national level data on the number of meals eaten per day and dietary diversity as well as food sources, consumption coping strategies and livelihoods activities. The Report concluded that the food security situation of the urban poor had increased since 2006 as a result of "high food prices, pricing of basic commodities in foreign currency, low cash withdrawal limits and high utility bills." At the same time, there are grounds for scepticism that 80% of poor urban households in Harare were food secure in 2006 and that nearly 70% were still food secure in 2009. The main problem, it appears, is that the measures used to determine if a household was food secure or insecure did not adequately capture the situation on the ground. In late 2008, at around the same time as the ZimVAC study, AFSUN conducted its own assessment of household food insecurity in Harare, using a different methodology for capturing food insecurity. The AFSUN results show much higher levels of food insecurity in the city.

3. METHODOLOGY

Due to resources and time constraints, the AFSUN survey did not sample the urban population of Harare as a whole. As in other participating cities, the focus of the study was the food security of poor urban households. The survey was implemented in three residential areas: Mabvuku, Tafara and Dzivarasekwa (Figure 1). Mabvuku and Tafara are neighbouring high density residential areas located about 20 kilometers to the east of Harare City Centre.

FIGURE 1: Location of Study Areas in Harare

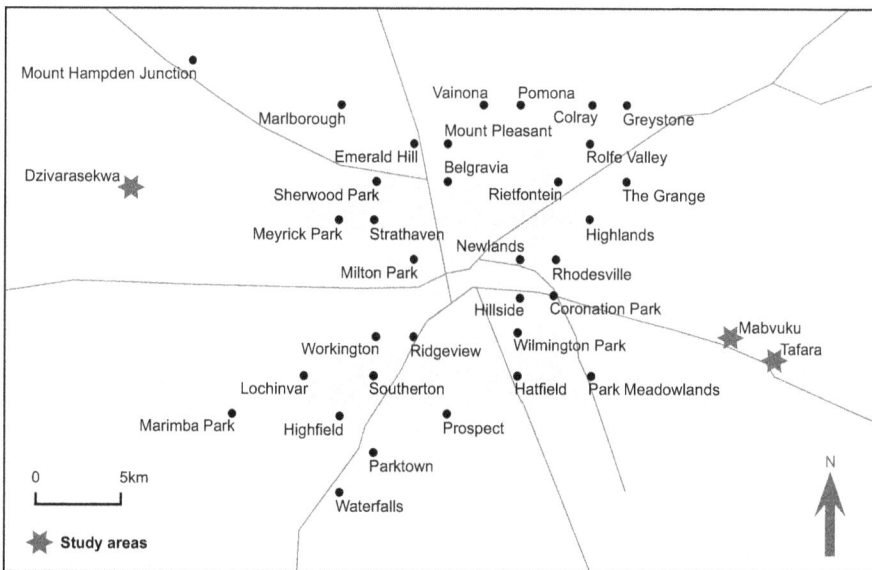

Source: Adapted from www.googlemaps.com

Mabvuku dates back to the 1950s when the white government decided to create a new residential area for blacks. The nucleus of the settlement was centered at Chizhanje, dominated by hostels meant to house migrant labour. This area was known as Old Mabvuku. New Mabvuku was added in 1972 as the original settlement was inadequate to accommodate a rapidly increasing migrant population. Tafara borders New Mabvuku and is also composed of an Old and a New Tafara. Both residential areas are inhabited by low income households, some of whom work in the industrial areas of Masasa or across the city in Willowvale and Graniteside. Dzivarasekwa, on the other hand, is located 20 kilometers in the west of the city. It is a later creation than the others, but is also inhabited by low-income households.

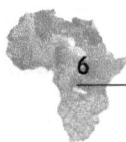

Sampling in Mabvuku, Tafara and Dzivarasekwa was essentially a two-stage process that involved the random identification of participating households and the selection, within chosen households, of the participating individuals. The surveys were conducted by six enumerators (three male and three female) from the University of Zimbabwe. A structured, pre-coded household questionnaire was used to collect data on household structure, livelihood strategies and food security. Because the survey was part of a larger scale survey that was being simultaneously carried out in eight other countries, the questionnaire had been standardized to allow for comparisons to be made between the countries in the region. The questionnaire was designed to capture information on household demographic characteristics, poverty data, income and expenditure patterns, household food insecurity experiences, dietary diversity information and household coping mechanisms.

The standardized questionnaire was administered to a total of 462 households across the survey areas. In the process, information relating to 2,572 people within these households was gathered (Table 1). While the average household size in the city was 5.6, and the median was 5.0, there was a wide range with the smallest being single-person households and the largest a household of 16 people. Fifty six percent of the households had 1-5 members and 42% had 6-10 members. Only 2% had more than 10 members in the household.

TABLE 1: Sample and Household Size	
Total number of households sampled	462
Total sample population	2,572
Average HH size	5.6
Median HH size	5.0
Smallest HH size	1
Largest HH size	16

As in the other 10 cities in which the survey was conducted, AFSUN used four measures of food security which have been developed, tested and refined by the Food and Nutrition Technical Assistance (FANTA) project over a number of years.[17] These included (a) the Household Food Insecurity Access Scale (HFIAS); (b) the Household Food Insecurity Access Prevalence Indicator (HFIAP); (c) the Household Dietary Diversity Score (HDDS); and (d) the Months of Adequate Household Food Provisioning (MAHFP) measure:

Household Food Insecurity Access Scale (HFIAS): The HFIAS score is a continuous measure of the degree of food insecurity in the household in the month prior to the survey.[18] An HFIAS score is calculated for each household based on answers to nine 'frequency-of-occurrence' questions.) The minimum score is 0 and the maximum is 27. The higher the score, the more food insecurity the household experienced. The lower the score, the less the food insecurity experienced.

Household Food Insecurity Access Prevalence Indicator (HFIAP): The HFIAP indicator categorizes households into four levels of household food insecurity: food secure, and mild, moderately and severely food insecure.[19] Households are categorized as increasingly food insecure as they respond affirmatively to more severe conditions and/or experience those conditions more frequently.

Household Dietary Diversity Scale (HDDS): Dietary diversity refers to how many food groups are consumed within the household over a given period.[20] The maximum number, based on the FAO classification of food groups for Africa, is 12. An increase in the average number of different food groups consumed provides a quantifiable measure of improved household food access. In general, any increase in household dietary diversity reflects an improvement in the household's diet.

Months of Adequate Household Food Provisioning Indicator (MAHFP): The MAHFP indicator captures changes in the household's ability to ensure that food is available above a minimum level all year round.[21] Households are asked to identify in which months (during the past 12 months) they did not have access to sufficient food to meet their household needs.

4. HOUSEHOLD CHARACTERISTICS

Zimbabwe is dominated by a patriarchal system where men are normally considered the de facto heads of household. Over the last decade there has been an increase in the number of households headed by females. ZimVAC's 2011 survey of 2,848 urban households throughout the country, for example, found that 68% of households were male-headed and 32% were female-headed.[22] This is higher than the 2008 AFSUN sample, where 23% of households were female-headed (Table 2). The increase in female-headed households is partly a function of migration dynamics in which males are more likely to make the first move to neighbouring

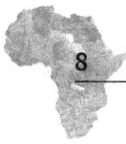

countries in search of work. Although some migrants later send for their families, this leaves an increasing number of females in charge of households. Only 8% of the households were male-centred (with no female partner or spouse). Nearly 40% were male-headed nuclear households and 32% were male-headed extended family households.

Household heads were generally fairly young: 12% were in their twenties, 30% were in their thirties and 21% were in their forties. The age profile of the entire sample was extremely youthful, with nearly half of the household members under the age of 20 (and 22% less than 10) (Figure 2). Nearly 70% were under the age of 30 and 82% were under the age of 40. The proportion of elderly was very small. The general age profile of household heads and household members certainly seems to bear the imprint of the HIV and AIDS epidemic which has significantly reduced life expectancy in Zimbabwe.[23] With 46% of the surveyed population aged below the age of 20 – and 57% being sons and daughters and grand-children – the implications for household food security are immediately obvious.[24] Although children do participate in income-generating activity (particularly in the informal economy), the majority are in school.

FIGURE 2: Age and Sex of Household Heads and Members

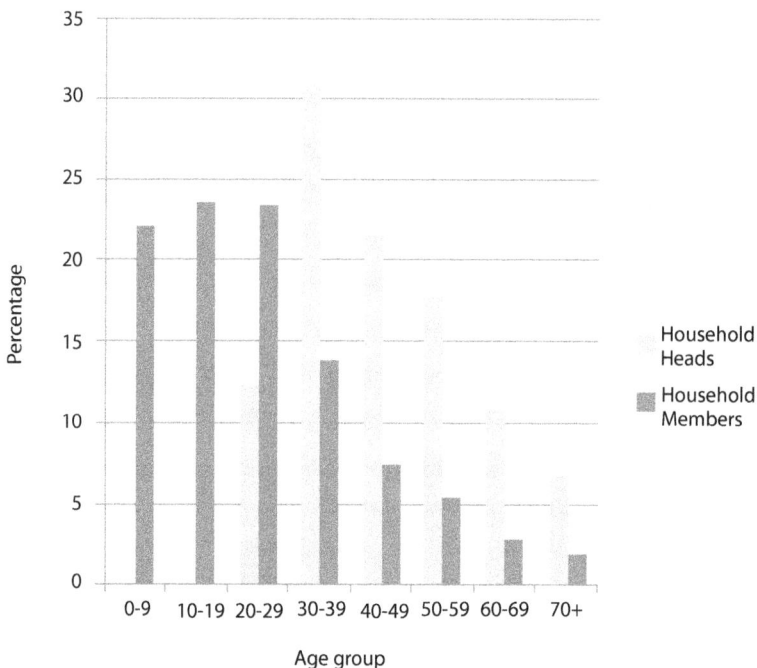

Household heads made up 18% of the total household membership, spouses 13% and children and grandchildren (57%) (Table 2). Other household members included brothers and sisters of the household head (5%), parents and grandparents (1%) and other relatives (6%). Less than 1% were unrelated orphans, foster children or adoptees. This suggests that in Harare at least, insofar as families look after orphans, they are generally members of their own extended families. Overall, there were more females in the total sample population (53%) compared to males (47%), another indication of the impact of migration.

TABLE 2: Household Members' Relationship to Household Heads			
		N	%
Relationship to Head	Head	462	18.0
	Spouse/partner	324	12.6
	Son/daughter	1,121	43.6
	Adopted/foster child/orphan	9	0.3
	Father/mother	19	0.7
	Brother/sister	124	4.8
	Grandchild	349	13.6
	Grandparent	4	0.2
	Son/daughter-in-law	47	1.8
	Other relative	105	4.1
	Non-relative	8	0.3
Total		2,572	100.0

The survey found that 40% of the adult population were employed full-time and another 14% were employed part-time or in casual work (Table 3). However, these figures include both formal and informal employment and it is likely that the vast majority of those who reported full-time employment were working in the informal economy. This would definitely have been the case for those in part-time or casual work. In 2004, the ILO calculated that Zimbabwe had 710,015 people (or 37%) working in informal enterprises and 1,200,549 (or 63%) working in formal enterprises.[25] In 2008, formal sector employment was estimated to have shrunk to 480,000.[26] At the height of the economic crisis, the proportion working in informal enterprises would easily have exceeded those in formal employment. Formal sector unemployment in Zimbabwe was estimated at over 90% in early 2009, for example.[27] Informal employment was "often survivalist in nature as people have no other option but to work, even if returns are meagre."[28] Despite this, as many as 43% of the adult population in the survey were not working at all, and nearly 30% had actually given up searching for work.

TABLE 3: Work Status of the Sample Population		
	N	%
Employed		
Full-Time	633	40.0
Part-Time/Casual	217	14.0
Status Unknown	21	1.3
Unemployed		
Looking for Work	226	14.0
Not Looking for Work	463	29.0
Status Unknown	39	2.0
Total	1,599	100.0

5. HOUSEHOLD POVERTY

5.1 Income Sources

In mid–2008, with inflation running at over 200 million percent and up to 80% of the population surviving on less than US$2 per day, Zimbabwe "had become a world leader in creating poverty."[29] Urban households required cash income to pay for their food as well as other essential services such as housing, transport and electricity. In a stable economic environment, with high levels of formal employment, households might have been able to survive on a single income source. In the highly volatile economic environment of 2008, a single income source was generally inadequate. The survey found that over three quarters of the households were relying on more than one income source for survival and as many as 27% had four or more sources (Table 4).

TABLE 4: Number of Income Sources		
No. of Income Sources	N	%
0	30	6
1	112	24
2	122	26
3	71	15
4 or More	124	27
Not Known	3	1
Total	492	100

Fifty five percent of households indicated that they received income from formal and informal wage work by household members and another 32%

acquired income from casual or part-time work. Other significant sources of income included remittances (12% of households) and rent (9% of households). On the other hand, it is striking how few of the households derived any income from the sale of agricultural produce grown in Harare (less than 2% of households) or grown in the rural areas and transferred to town (less than 1.5% of households). Only 2% of households received income from social grants (such as pensions).

In 2005, Lloyd Sachikonye characterised Operation Murambatsvina as a tsunami which swept away the urban informal economy of cities like Harare:

> For many of the poor and those in the informal economy in Zimbabwe, the tsunami was made up of waves and waves of demolitions on enterprises that they had slowly and painstakingly built over the years. It was a relentless onslaught from the authorities with armed police at the frontline. The tsunami swept away small tuck shops, carpentry shops, hair saloons, repair shops, small industrial establishments, brick foundries, vending sites and grinding mills to name a few. These small and medium scale enterprises (SMEs) had multiplied steadily to provide livelihoods to millions as well as to the thousands who had been retrenched due to the economic structural adjustment programme (ESAP) and the economic decline in the post-2000 period respectively.[30]

Others have shown how the informal economy quickly recovered after this draconian attempt to obliterate it from the urban landscape.[31] Three years after the tsunami, this survey showed that the informal economy was booming again. As many as 42% of households obtained income from informal economy activity (Table 5).

The average household income for the survey sample was the equivalent of R1,551 per month and the median was only R800 per month (Table 5). The mean income for wage work was a mere R636 per month, less than for informal business activity (R1,284), casual work (R782) and remittances (R757). The mean income for those with a formal business or selling urban agricultural produce was higher, but the number of households in each case was very small.

The conversion from Zimbabwean Dollars to South African Rand (or even to USD) makes it easier to comprehend how little income households were generating at the time of the survey.[32] However, this should be seen as illustrative rather than definitive since inflation was soaring and the exchange rate was changing almost daily at this time. There was also a significant difference between the official and black market exchange rates.[33] Food prices were also extremely high and volatile, making it extremely difficult for respondents to clearly know the purchasing power of the income they did earn.

TABLE 5: Sources of Household Income			
	N	% of Total Households	Mean Monthly Income (ZAR)
Wage work	253	55	636
Informal business	195	42	1,284
Casual work	150	32	782
Remittances (money)	56	12	757
Rent	41	9	143
Formal business	14	3	2,218
Pension/disability/allowance/grant	10	2	56
Sale of urban farm products	8	2	814
Sale of rural farm products	6	1	603
Gifts	6	1	157
Aid (cash)	1	<1	50
All sources combined			1,552
Note: More than one answer permitted N = 462			

FIGURE 3: Household Monthly Income (ZAR)

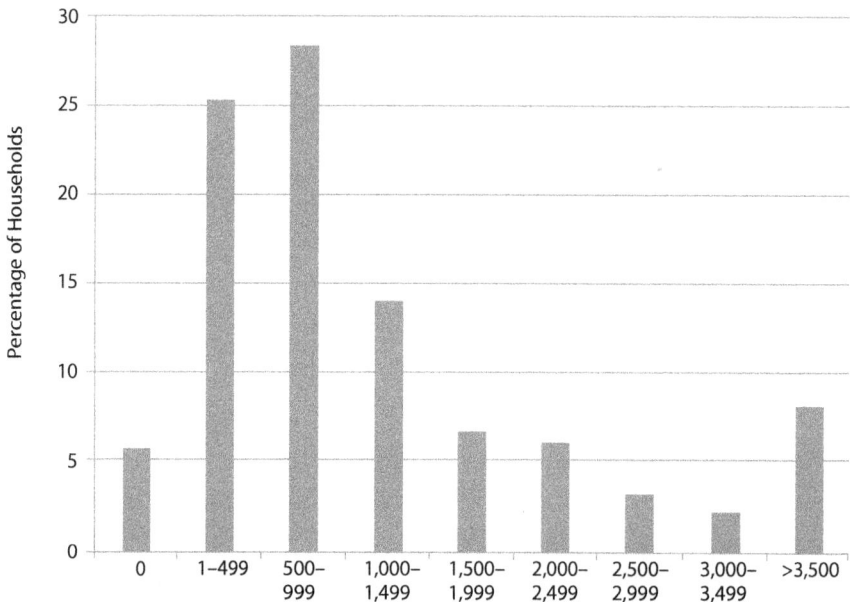

5.2 Household Expenditures

The expenditure patterns of surveyed households clearly indicate that they were trying to survive under extreme conditions. In the urban environment, most households tend to purchase the bulk of their food. The survey showed that 94% of households were purchasing food. Food and groceries constituted the single largest expenditure (averaging R472 per month) (Table 6). Other major draws on income were housing and utilities (although the actual amounts spent were much smaller than for food). Nearly 60% of households had education-related costs which reflects the large number of children in surveyed households but also the premium placed on education, even in trying circumstances. Other indicators of the desperate times for many households included a very low savings rate (only 4% of households were saving anything) and the fact that 20% were using income to make more income by purchasing and re-selling goods. Those households were spending an average of R1,122 per month on purchase for resale. Intermittent power cuts meant that nearly 60% of households were forced to purchase alternative fuels such as firewood, paraffin and charcoal. Finally, only 6% of the households were remitting cash (presumably to family members in rural areas). This aspect of the Zimbabwean crisis has received insufficient attention as remitting levels were much higher in the past.

TABLE 6: Household Expenditure Categories			
	N	% of Total Households	Mean Monthly Expenditure (ZAR)
Food and Groceries	428	94	472
Housing	413	90	60
Utilities	411	90	27
Fuel	266	58	81
Education	263	58	40
Transportation	164	36	243
Medical expenses	120	26	58
Goods purchased to resell	98	21	1,122
Funeral costs	42	9	90
Remittances	30	6	109
Savings	20	4	722
Debt service/repayment	15	3	53
Home-based care	11	2	121
Insurance	7	1	21
Note: More than one answer permitted N=456			

5.3 Lived Poverty

In the context of massive inflation, income-based measures of poverty are particularly unreliable as a guide to the prevalence and experience of economic hardship. To capture other dimensions of poverty, the AFSUN survey used the Afrobarometer's Lived Poverty Index (LPI).[34] The LPI measures how frequently people self-report going without certain basic necessities such as food, clean water, medicine, fuel to cook food and an income over the course of the previous year. An LPI score is calculated for each household in the range 0.00 (complete satisfaction of basic needs) to 4.00 (always without basic needs). The average LPI score for Harare was 2.2. This was much higher than for any other city in the AFSUN survey (Figure 4) and indicates that the Harare households failed to satisfy their basic needs more frequently than those in any other city. Only 10% of the Harare households never or seldom went without the basket of basic needs (Table 7).

FIGURE 4: Comparison of LPI Scores in Harare and Other Cities

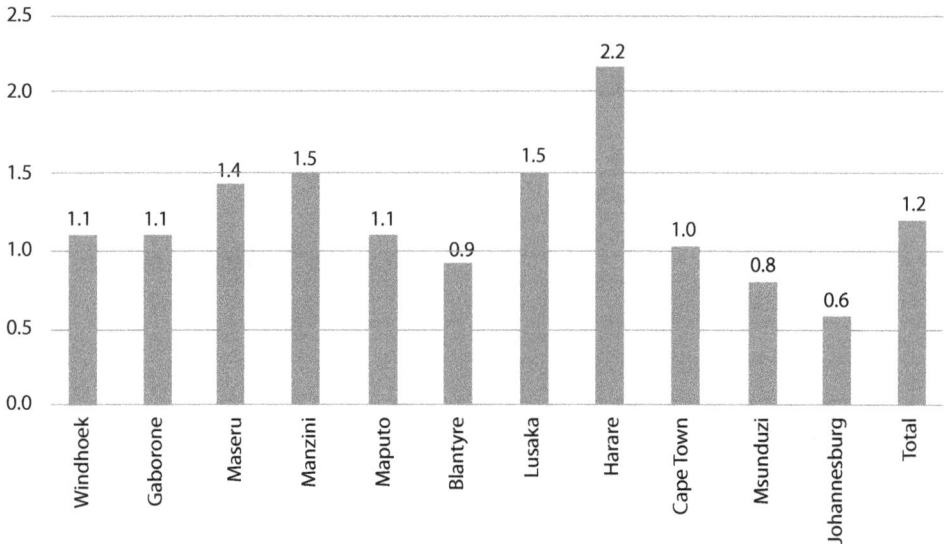

TABLE 7: Lived Poverty Index (LPI) Categories in Harare		
	No.	%
0.00-1.00 (Never to Seldom Without)	42	9.8
1.01-2.00 (Seldom to Sometimes Without)	152	35.3
2.01-3.00 (Sometimes to Often Without)	193	44.9
3.01-4.00 (Often to Always Without)	43	10.0
Total	430	100.0

In the year prior to the survey, over 60% of households reported that they had frequently gone without clean water and electricity and only 8% and 1% respectively said they had never done so (Table 8). These responses are consistent with the city's constant power cuts and sanitation problems that led to the major cholera outbreak in 2008-9.[35] Almost 60% of households reported that they had always/many times gone without a cash income in the previous year and only 11% said they had never gone without a cash income. These responses were consistent with reports that formal unemployment exceeded 80% by 2008. Interestingly, given the importance of food purchase, the equivalent figures for food were 40% going without always/many times and only 19% never going without.

TABLE 8: Frequency of Going without Basic Needs			
	Gone Without Many Times/ Always %	Gone Without Once or Twice/ Several Times %	Never Gone Without %
Enough food to eat	40	40	19
Enough clean water for home use	67	37	8
Medicine or medical treatment	40	37	23
Electricity in home	61	37	1
Enough fuel to cook food	32	56	12
A cash income	59	30	11

6. LEVELS OF HOUSEHOLD FOOD INSECURITY

As noted above, the Household Food Insecurity Access Scale (HFIAS) assigns all households a score on a scale between 0 (least food insecure) and 27 (most food insecure). The HFIAS shows that surveyed households in Harare were amongst the most food insecure in the region. The range in Harare was from 0 to 27 with a mean of 14.7 and a median of 16.0. Comparatively speaking, only households in Manzini, Swaziland, had similar levels of food insecurity (mean of 14.9 and median of 14.7). All of the other cities in the region had lower mean and median HFIAS scores than Harare (Table 9).

TABLE 9: HFIAS Scores in Harare Compared to Other Cities			
	Mean	Median	N
Manzini, Swaziland	14.9	14.7	489
Harare, Zimbabwe	14.7	16.0	454
Maseru, Lesotho	12.8	13.0	795
Lusaka, Zambia	11.5	11.0	386
Msunduzi, South Africa	11.3	11.0	548
Gaborone, Botswana	10.8	11.0	391
Cape Town, South Africa	10.7	11.0	1,026
Maputo, Mozambique	10.4	10.0	389
Windhoek, Namibia	9.3	9.0	442
Blantyre, Malawi	5.3	3.7	431
Johannesburg, South Africa	4.7	1.5	976

The HFIAP makes a finer distinction between food secure and food insecure households by allocating each household to one of four food security groups based on their HFIAP score: (a) food secure; (b) mildly food
insecure; (c) moderately food insecure; and (d) severely food insecure.
The surveyed households in Harare scored worse on the HFIAP indicator
than those in any other city (Table 10).

TABLE 10: HFIAP Scores in Harare Compared to Other Cities				
	Food Secure %	Mildly Food Insecure %	Moderately Food Insecure %	Severely Food Insecure %
Harare, Zimbabwe	2	3	24	72
Lusaka, Zambia	4	3	24	69
Maseru, Lesotho	5	6	25	65
Maputo, Mozambique	5	9	32	54
Manzini, Swaziland	6	3	13	79
Msunduzi, South Africa	7	6	27	60
Gaborone, Botswana	12	6	19	63
Cape Town, South Africa	15	5	12	68
Windhoek, Namibia	18	5	14	63
Blantyre, Malawi	34	15	30	21
Johannesburg, South Africa	44	14	15	27

In general, in every city except Johannesburg and Blantyre, less than 20%
of households fell into the food secure category. Only 2% of the Harare
households were food secure, the lowest proportion of all eleven cities.
Contrariwise, Harare had the second highest proportion of severely food

insecure households (72% after Manzini at 79%). Harare households were not significantly more food insecure than those in a number of other cities, however. In every city except Johannesburg, over 60% of households were severely food insecure. Poor urban communities throughout the region were therefore experiencing the kinds of livelihood pressures and food insecurity struggles faced by households in Zimbabwe.

The HDDS shows that dietary diversity was very poor for most of the surveyed households in Harare. As many as two thirds of the households (68%) had eaten from five or fewer of the twelve different FAO food groups in the 24 hours prior to the survey (Figure 5). Nearly a third (29%) of the households had eaten from three groups or less. Dietary diversity was worse in Harare than in all other cities. The comparative figures for the eleven survey cities as a whole were 48% (five or less groups) and 23% (three or less groups). Only 33% of Harare households ate food from 6 or more food groups compared with 51% of households in the regional sample.

FIGURE 5: Household Dietary Diversity Scores

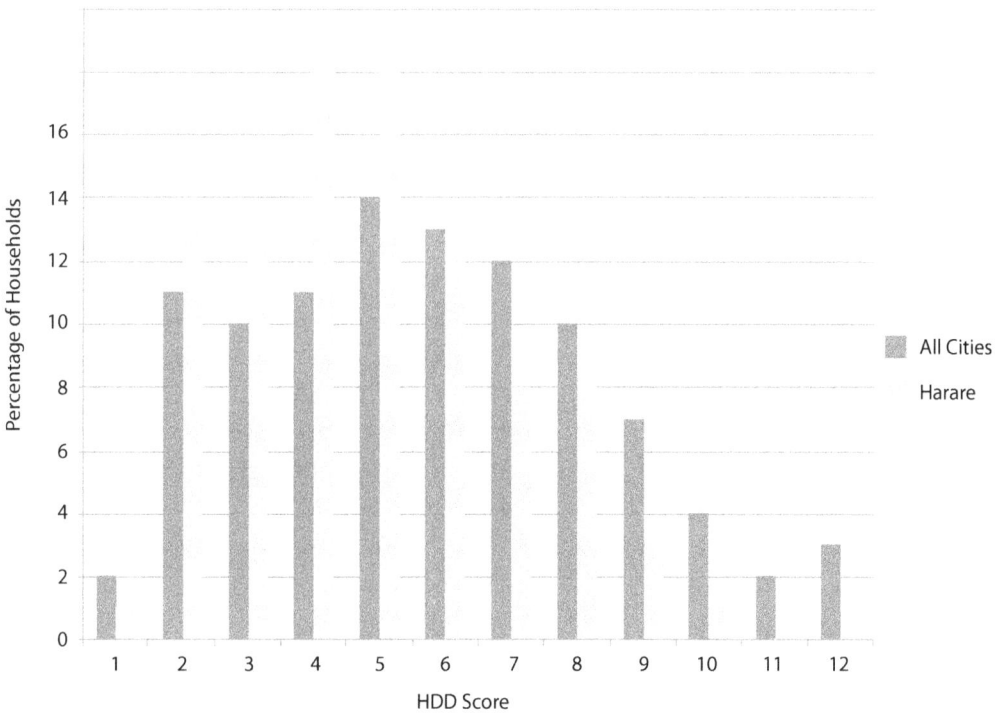

All Cities, N=6,453
Harare, N=454

Narrow household diets reflect a deeper food insecurity problem that goes beyond the issue of food availability. But, what kinds of foods did these households consume? Most ate cereals or foods made from grains, vegetables, sugar and foods made with oil, butter, or fat (Table 11). Less than 20% of households consumed fruit, meat or poultry, eggs or dairy.

TABLE 11: Food Groups Eaten By Households		
	N	%
1 Cereals (foods made from grain)	455	99
2 Roots or tubers	57	12
3 Vegetables	423	92
4 Fruits	70	15
5 Meat, poultry or offal	103	22
6 Eggs	40	9
7 Fresh or dried fish or shellfish	81	18
8 Foods made from beans, peas, lentils or nuts	84	18
9 Cheese, yoghurt, milk or other milk products	54	12
10 Foods made with oil, fat or butter	261	56
11 Sugar or honey	295	64
12 Other foods	284	62

Another aspect of food insecurity is the regularity and consistency of access to food. The Months of Adequate Household Food Provisioning (MAHFP) indicator shows that about 92% of the households in the survey had experienced some months of inadequate food provisioning during the year preceding the survey. The months of greatest inadequacy were from June to October (Figure 6). During these months, more than 50% of households experienced food shortages. In the month of September, three quarters of households did not have sufficient food to eat. The pattern of food shortages seems to follow the agricultural seasons in the country. More households reported being adequately provisioned during the country's agricultural season (November-May) while severe shortages were reported for the dry winter months (July-October). Food prices (especially cereals) also tended to be lower during the agricultural season. In addition, strong rural-urban linkages and high levels of urban agriculture increased the seasonality of the urban food supply for poor households.

FIGURE 6: Months of Inadequate Food Provisioning of Households

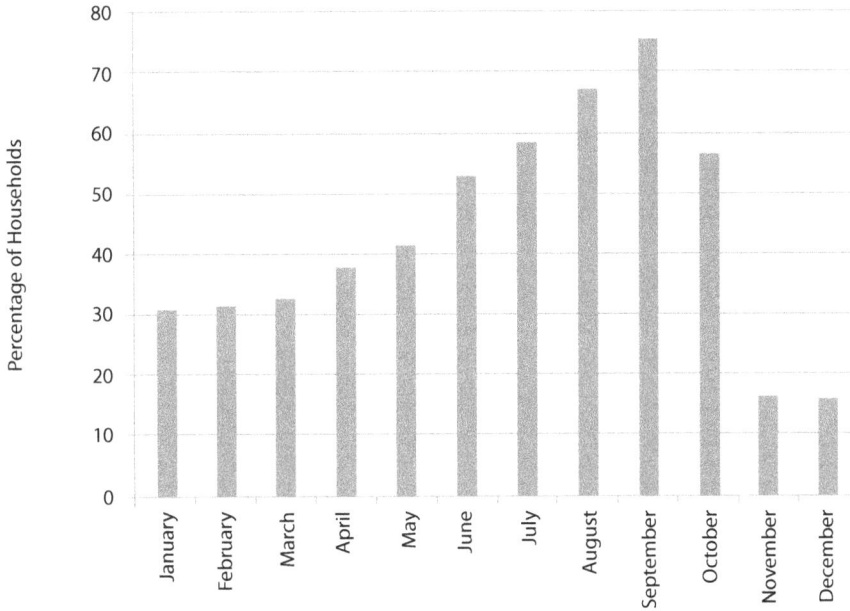

7. DETERMINANTS OF FOOD INSECURITY

7.1 Household Size and Structure

Although household size is not necessarily a significant determinant of food security status in urban areas, it does have a considerable impact if household incomes are low and do not differ substantially. In such circumstances, larger household size would mean greater food insecurity as more mouths rely on meagre income to survive. In normal economic times, the addition of (adult) household members has the potential to increase household income and therefore the food security of all household members. In the region as a whole, the survey did not find a strong relationship between household size and degree of food insecurity.[36] In Harare, however, with unemployment at over 80% and household income from all sources being extremely constrained, we anticipated a stronger relationship between household size and food security.

The survey found that there was a slight tendency for larger households to be more food insecure: for example, 69% of households with 1-5 members were severely food insecure compared with 76% of households with 6-10 members and 90% of households with more than 10 members (Table 12).

However, the difference was not statistically significant primarily because the absolute number of food insecure households in the sample is so high. Additionally, the number of households with more than 10 members is relatively small. A similar observation can be made about household structure. Although proportionally more female-centred households are severely food insecure, the sheer number of households in each category that are severely food insecure renders any differences between types of households statistically insignificant.

TABLE 12: Household Food Security by Household Size and Structure					
	Food Secure %	Mildly Food Insecure %	Moderately Food Insecure %	Severely Food Insecure %	N
No. of Persons					
1–5	2	4	25	69	255
6–10	1	1	22	76	188
> 10	0	0	10	90	11
Household Type					
Female-Centred	2	2	18	78	102
Male-Centred	3	3	21	73	33
Nuclear	2	2	25	71	171
Extended	1	4	28	67	148

7.2 Household Poverty

The relationship between food security and the general income poverty of the survey population is immediately apparent. Cross-tabulating food security with income terciles, for example, shows that while no households in the lowest tercile were food secure, only 4% in the upper tercile were food secure. Income does, however, have an influence on the severity of food insecurity. While 86% of households in the lowest tercile were severely food insecure, the figure dropped to 63% of those in the upper tercile, a statistically significant difference (Table 13). The relationship between poverty and food insecurity was even stronger with the Lived Poverty Index (LPI). Nearly 10% of the households in the highest category (never to seldom without various basic needs) were food secure and 34% were severely food insecure. The equivalent scores for the lowest category (often or always without) were 0% and 93%. In general, as the LPI score improves so does the food security status of the household.

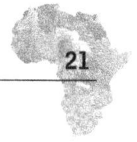

TABLE 13: Household Food Security Status by Poverty Measures

	Food Secure %	Mildly Food Insecure %	Moderately Food Insecure %	Severely Food Insecure %	N
Income Terciles					
Poorest (<R500)	0	1	13	86	116
Less Poor(R500–1,199	1	3	25	71	161
Least Poor (R1,200+)	4	4	29	63	150
Lived Poverty Index					
3.01-4.00 (Often–Always Without)	0	0	7	93	42
2.01-3.00 (Sometimes–Often Without)	0	0	17	83	193
1.01-2.00 (Seldom–Sometimes Without)	2	5	30	63	146
0.00-1.00 (Seldom–Never Without)	9	12	45	34	42

As a general rule, the poorer the household, the greater the proportion of its income that is spent on food purchase. The surveyed households in Zimbabwe said they spend, on average, 62% of their income on food. Not only is this an extremely high figure, it is well ahead of all the individual cities in the AFSUN survey and the regional average of 50% (Table 14).

TABLE 14: Proportion of Income Spent on Food

	N	% of Income Spent on Food
Harare, Zimbabwe	417	62
Cape Town, South Africa	985	55
Lusaka, Zambia	357	54
Maputo, Mozambique	314	53
Msunduzi, South Africa	456	52
Johannesburg, South Africa	886	49
Blantyre, Malawi	424	46
Maseru, Lesotho	628	46
Gaborone, Botswana	374	46
Manzini, Swaziland	345	42
Windhoek, Namibia	430	36
Total	5,616	50

7.3 Rising Food Prices

Food price increases in Harare in 2008 can be attributed to increasing global food prices and internal inflation. It was normal, particularly between July and October 2008 when inflation peaked, for the price of food to increase threefold in a single day. Between 2007 and 2008, international and regional food prices rose to unprecedented levels.[37] Zimbabwe had become a major food importer over the previous decade, which left it particularly vulnerable to price increases. The price of the food staple, maize, rose far more steeply in Harare in 2008 than it did in other Southern African cities (Figure 7). Such price rises were particularly devastating for poor urban households. Only 3% of the surveyed households noted that they had avoided going without food because of price increases in the previous six months. Some 11% of the households reported going without food about once a month and 16% once a week, while over two-thirds of the households were fairing much worse. Over a third (38%) said they were going without food due to price increases more than once a week and 32% said they were affected every day.

FIGURE 7: Maize Prices in Urban Southern Africa, 2007-9

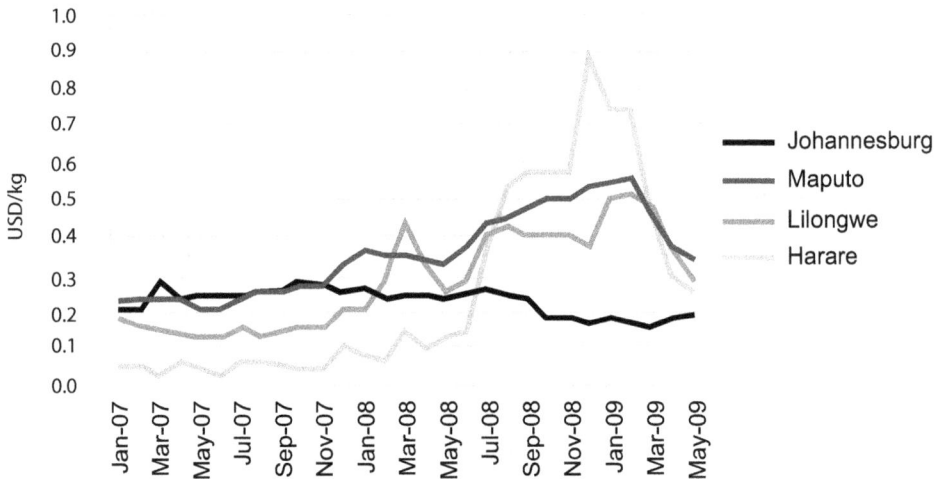

Food price increases also had a major impact on dietary diversity. While only 18% households said they had gone without vegetables due to price increases in the previous six months, more than 50% of households had gone without every other food group due to price increases (Figure 8). The most inaccessible foodstuffs were milk and milk products and eggs (over 80% went without); meat, poultry, roots, tubers and fruit (over 75%); and foods made with oil, fat or butter and fish (over 60%). As many as 57% of households had gone without staple cereals due to price increases as well.

FIGURE 8: Types of Food Not Consumed Due to Price Increases

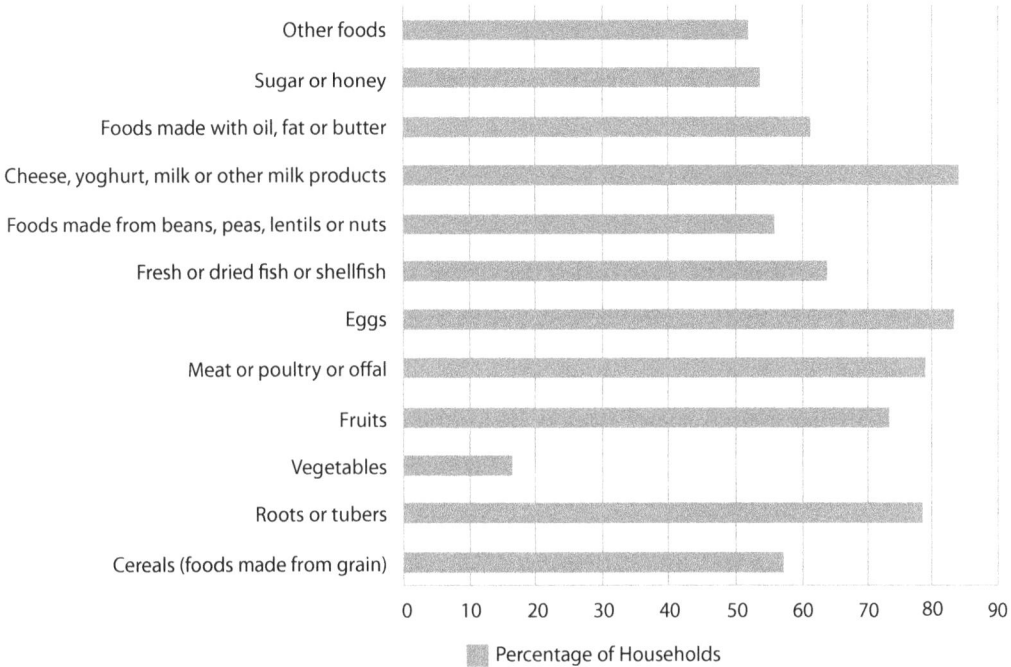

Percentage of Households

The frequency of going without food due to price increases in the previous six months was strongly correlated with food insecurity. A surprisingly high 51% of those who said they had not gone without food due to food price increases were also severely food insecure on the HFIAP scale (Table 15). This suggests that these households, though very food insecure, were relying on non-market sources for some or all of their food. At the same time, as the frequency of going without food increased, so did the proportion of households who were severely food insecure. Thus, 73% of those households that had gone without food "several times" were severely food insecure while 97% of those who said they "always" went without food were also severely food insecure on the HFIAP scale.

TABLE 15: Household Food Insecurity and Frequency of Going Without Food Due to Price Increases					
	Food Secure %	Mildly Food Insecure %	Moderately Food Insecure %	Severely Food Insecure %	N
Never	6	12	31	51	86
Just once or twice	0	4	48	48	71
Several times	2	0	25	73	109
Many times	1	0	12	87	145
Always	0	0	3	97	36

8. SOURCES OF HOUSEHOLD FOOD

8.1 Surviving on Informal Food

Poor households in Southern African cities obtain their food from a variety of formal and informal sources. Supermarkets are more important than the informal economy in some cities and the reverse is true in others. What is clear is that these are the dominant sources of food for households in most cities.[38] In the eleven cities as a whole, 79% of households indicated that they source food from supermarkets and 70% that they do so from the informal economy. Also important in some cities are smaller formal-sector outlets including corner stores, grocers, butcheries and fast-food outlets. In total, 68% of households said that they use these outlets. Food transfers from rural households are important in some cities (such as Windhoek and Lusaka) but not in others (such as the South African cities). Urban agriculture is important in cities like Blantyre and insignificant in cities such as Windhoek. Overall, however, only 21% of households produce any of their own food.

Food sourcing in Harare differed significantly from the regional picture (Figure 9). The strategies used by poor urban households to buy food clearly reflect the precarious social and economic situation prevailing in the city at the time:

- Supermarkets were far less important as a source of food than in all other cities. Only 30% of households sourced food from supermarkets, compared to a regional average of 79%. Price controls by government made it difficult for the supermarkets to source and sell their products at realistic profit margins, and most of them have either closed or were operating at very low capacity. Harare is well-served by supermarkets but the supermarket shelves themselves were often bare;

- Small formal sector shops were having even greater difficulty getting stock at this time. They were patronized by only 17% of surveyed households in Harare, compared with the regional average of 68%;

- On the other hand, virtually all households (98%) were sourcing food through informal channels (compared to the regional average of 70%). Much of this food was imported from South Africa by informal traders and sold on to urban households through informal markets, by street vendors and house-to-house.[39] In other words, but for the informal economy which the government tried to destroy in 2005, the food insecurity of urban households would have been completely catastrophic. Nearly 80% of households obtained food from informal sources at least five days a week, suggesting that they were buying in small quantities that necessitated more frequent patronage (Figure 10). In this way, they could negotiate whatever smaller amounts of food their money would buy.

• Other major differences between Harare and other cities included food borrowing and informal food transfers from the rural areas (both signs of desperation). Levels of participation in urban agriculture were also significant as desperate households tried to eke out food on their own land or in public spaces (see below).

FIGURE 9: Food Sources in Harare and Other Cities

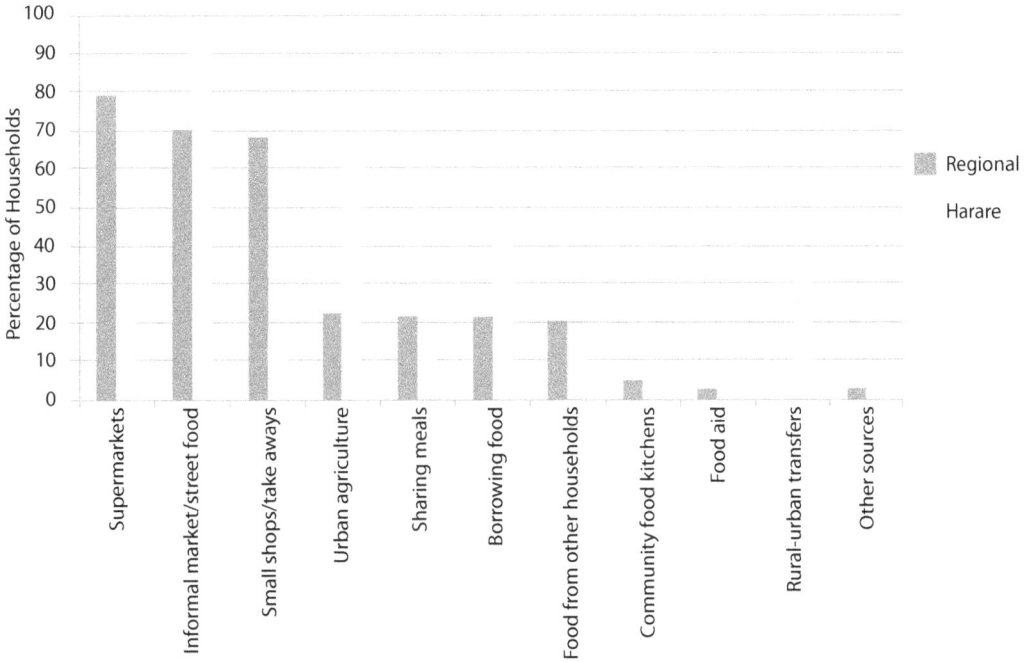

FIGURE 10: Frequency of Patronage of Food Sources

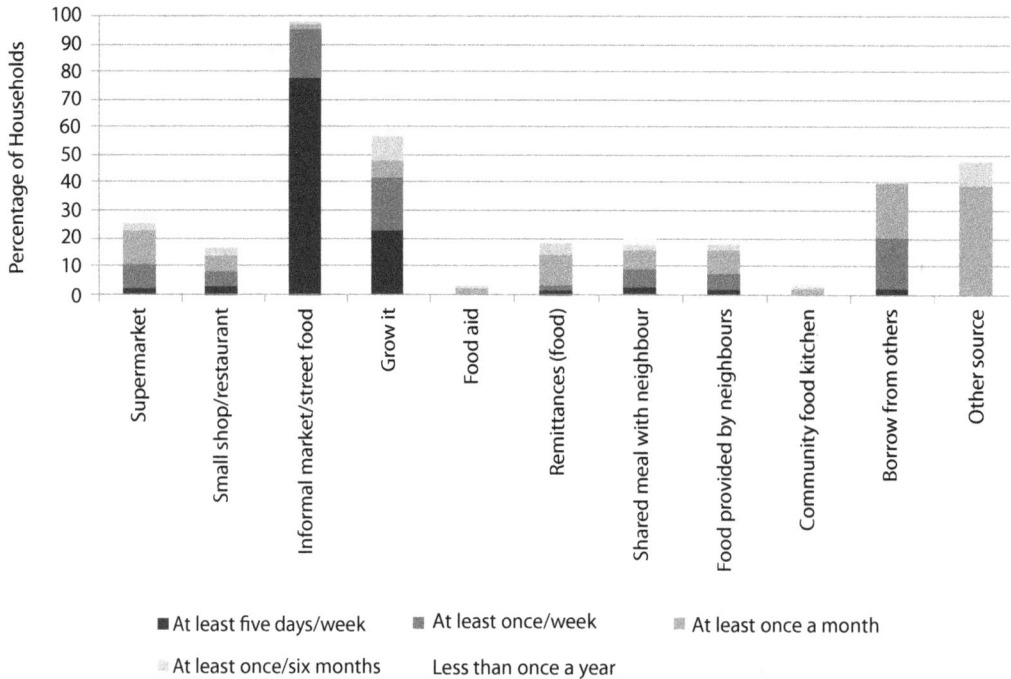

- At least five days/week
- At least once/week
- At least once a month
- At least once/six months
- Less than once a year

8.2 Urban Agriculture

In the 1990s, economic hardship forced those households who could access land to try and supplement their food basket through home production.[40] By 2008, urban agriculture had become ubiquitous throughout the city:

> The profile of urban cultivators has changed over time as a result of the economic downturn. In the past, it was mainly the poorer citizens who used open spaces (off-plot) for crop production. But now there is competition amongst people of all income brackets. People with higher incomes, who could afford to buy their own food, say five years ago, now have found their incomes so eroded by inflation that they cannot afford to buy all food provisions. They have to resort to urban agriculture to supplement their diets and their incomes. It is now common to see families from high-income residential areas cultivating open space areas that used to be cultivated by their employees and residents from lower-income areas.[41]

Toriro estimates that there were as many as 500,000 urban farmers in Harare in 2008. This survey found that 60% of households were engaged in urban agriculture (growing crops or keeping livestock) and that 40% relied on home production for food at least once a week (Figure 10). Harare was second only to Blantyre of the eleven cities surveyed in terms of the

degree of participation in urban agriculture (Figure 11). However, only 6% of households derived any income from the sale of home produce, confirming that urban agriculture was not income-generating so much as a survival strategy for the vast majority of households.

FIGURE 11: Urban Agriculture in Southern African Cities

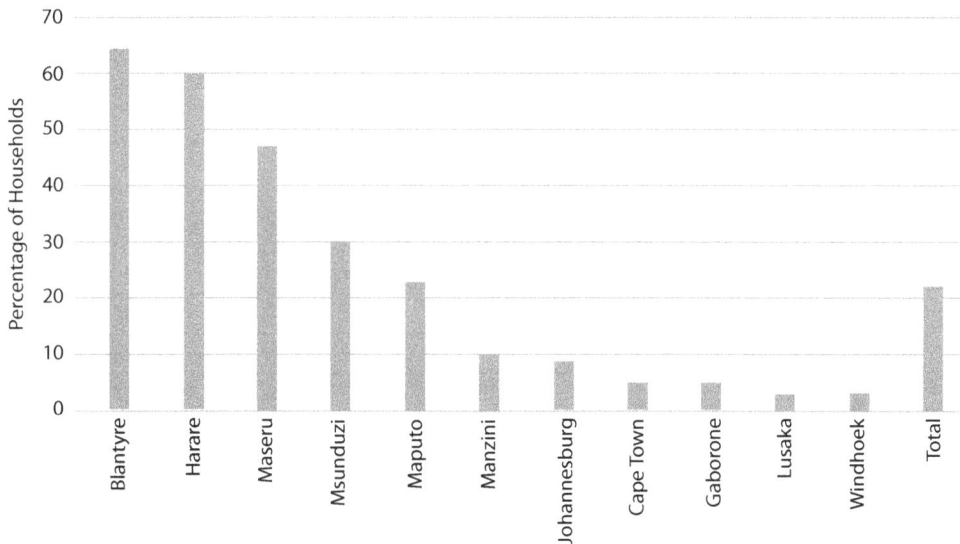

8.3 Informal Food Transfers

Food transfers proved to be important to the survival of many households in Harare. These transfers come from family or friends in the rural areas, other urban areas, or other countries where Zimbabwean migrants are now domiciled. Some urban households also maintain plots in the rural areas where they grow crops which they transfer to the city for their own consumption. A total of 192 surveyed households (or 42%) had received food transfers in the previous year (Table 16). Some 37% of these households received transfers from the rural areas, 43% from other urban areas and 20% from both rural and urban areas.

The most important type of food received was cereals, mostly maize and rapoko, which are staple crops in the country (Table 17). While urbanites used to get these cereals from the urban market, perennial food shortages in the city have forced them to obtain maize and rapoko directly from rural family and friends. Fresh vegetables, as well as the dried variety known locally as *mufushwa,* constituted 17% of the transfers and foods made from beans, peas, lentils or nuts, 15%. Transfers of fruit, meat and dairy were relatively unimportant.

TABLE 16: Transfers as Food Sources for Urban Households		
Source of Transfer	N	% of Households
Rural areas – Relatives	105	24
Rural areas – Friends	19	5
Urban areas – Relatives	92	21
Urban areas – Friends	48	11
Rural areas only	71	37
Urban areas only	82	43
Rural & urban areas	39	20
N	192	

TABLE 17: Type of Food Transferred from Rural Areas		
	N	%
Cereals (foods made from grain)	105	48
Roots or tubers	10	5
Vegetables	38	17
Fruits	6	3
Meat or poultry or offal	7	3
Eggs	2	1
Fresh or dried fish or shellfish	1	-
Foods made from beans, peas, lentils or nuts	33	15
Cheese, yoghurt, milk or other milk products	7	3
Foods made with oil, fat or butter	7	3
Sugar or honey	1	–
N	217	

Regardless of the nutrient content of the food transfers, households receiving food from the rural areas indicated that this food was vitally important for their survival (Table 18). About two-thirds of the households receiving food from rural areas (67%) indicated that the transfers were very important, while 16% viewed them as critical to their survival.

The picture that these responses paint underscores the critical role that transfers play in the survival of urban households in Harare. It is no wonder that the majority of the households receiving food (91%) indicate that the reason for this food is to help the household to feed itself (Table 19).

TABLE 18: Importance of Food Transfers		
	N	%
Not important at all	1	-
Somewhat important	6	3
Important	25	13
Very important	126	67
Critical to our survival	31	16
Total	189	100

TABLE 19: Reasons for Sending Food and its Uses in the Urban Area			
		N	%
Reasons for sending food	To help this household feed itself	184	91
	As gifts	18	9
	Other reason for sending food	1	-
	Total	203	100
Use of food	Eat it	188	89
	Sell it	6	3
	Give it away to friends/relatives	16	8
	Feed it to livestock (including chickens)	1	-
	Total	211	100
Selling of food	Sell on the street (hawker/vendor)	2	1
	Sell it from home	6	3
	Not applicable	186	96
	Total	194	100

9. CONCLUSION

The AFSUN Harare survey was implemented at a time when the entire country was experiencing acute food shortages. This report therefore provides a picture of the situation in Harare at its very worst. The city was literally under siege from a toxic mix of economic mismanagement, political crisis and policies that had turned the country from a net exporter to a massive formal and informal importer of food. The city was also recuperating from the government's 2005 attempt to obliterate the urban informal economy on which so many depended for their survival.

The AFSUN survey highlights a number of dimensions of urban food security at this time.

Firstly, the survey suggests that the 2006 and 2009 ZimVAC Urban Food Security Assessments underestimated the levels of poverty and food insecurity in Harare.[42] A significant proportion of households in the study areas were living in conditions of extreme poverty where they were unable to meet their everyday basic food requirements as well as other essential needs. The food insecurity access scales used by AFSUN showed that 72% of households were experiencing severe food insecurity and another 24% moderate food insecurity. Only 2% of households were food secure. This compares with the 2009 ZimVAC finding that only 33% of households in Harare were food insecure.[43] In part, the difference is a function of the different methodologies and measurements of food insecurity employed by AFSUN and ZimVAC. However, the AFSUN scales are well-tried international measures that have stood up to testing in a variety of comparative contexts and, as such, do seem to provide an accurate picture of the situation on the ground in 2008.[44]

The other possible source of difference is that the two surveys were conducted in different areas of the city and, in the case of the ZimVAC households surveyed, outside Harare in neighbouring Chitungwiza.[45] One of the areas sampled by ZimVAC was the low-income suburb of Epworth. Unfortunately, the ZimVAC report does not disaggregate the findings for Epworth. One of the authors of this report conducted a separate survey of Epworth in early 2009, however, and found an average HFIAS score that was very similar to that in the AFSUN survey.[46] The proportion of severely food insecure households was 59% and 31% were moderately food insecure. The proportion of food secure households was only 3%. This suggests that the situation may have been improving for some of the most food insecure households by mid-2009. At the same time, the Epworth figures for 2009 indicate much higher levels of food insecurity than the 2009 ZimVAC survey.

Secondly, the AFSUN survey provides considerable insights into the factors that increased the vulnerability of the urban poor to food insecurity at the height of the crisis. These mainly revolve around issues of poverty and unemployment which barred households from accessing sufficient income in order to meet their non-discretionary basic needs, especially for food. One of the questions that arises, therefore, is how different Harare was from other cities in the region? Were the urban poor of the poor neighbourhoods of Harare significantly worse off and more food insecure than those in other cities? On most measures of poverty, hardship and food insecurity, Harare was the most difficult city to be poor in in 2008. At the same time, the pressures and challenges facing the urban poor in Harare differed in degree rather than kind from those confronting the urban poor in other countries and cities. In other words, it is not possible

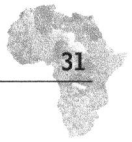

to simply "write off" the food insecurity of the urban poor in Harare as a function of the particular, even unique, constellation of economic and political crises affecting that country. Poor urban neighbourhoods throughout the region were suffering under a more generalised crisis of food insecurity.[47]

Thirdly, the survey showed the critical importance of the informal economy for many households in the city. Operation Murambatsvina was extremely disruptive and had a major impact on the livelihoods of many. Yet, only three years later, the informal economy had clearly "bounced back" and many households were participating out of necessity in order to make income and to access food. At a time when formal sector food supply chains were simply unable to make food available for purchase, the informal economy ensured that households with income could continue to access food.

Fourthly, a significant number of households in the survey were reliant on non-market channels for accessing food. Three in particular are worth highlighting: urban agriculture, rural-urban food transfers and social networks. Across the region, the AFSUN survey showed that urban agriculture was far less significant than conventional wisdom suggested.[48] However, in Harare, urban agriculture was a critical survival strategy.[49] Very few were actually selling and making income from home produce. Instead, faced with conditions of extreme food insecurity, they were consuming the food themselves. Rural-urban informal food transfers were also extremely important for a significant number of urban households. Potts has shown that urban households in Zimbabwe do maintain strong rural links.[50] By 2008, their ability to remit money to the rural areas had virtually dried up even as they began to rely more on their rural counterparts to help them survive in the city through food transfers.

Finally, the survey showed the importance of social networks and, in particular, the large number of households that were borrowing and lending food from each other. Informal social protection appears to have been a significant response to the crisis. On the other hand, the absence of formal safety nets for the urban poor was evident and suggests the need for far more attention to social protection as a mechanism for alleviating poverty and food insecurity in the urban areas of Zimbabwe.

The final question is whether food security in Harare has improved since the survey was undertaken. Using its methodology, ZimVAC has suggested that between 2009 and 2011, levels of food insecurity in Harare fell from 33% to only 13%.[51] Even allowing for the fact that their methodology may underestimate the extent of food insecurity in Harare, we can

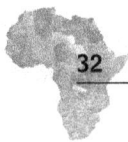

assume that there is some internal consistency between the 2009 and 2011 studies. This means that there is at least a testable hypothesis that levels of food insecurity have more than halved in the last 2-3 years. Whether a similar result would be obtained using the AFSUN methodology remains to be seen. However, a follow-up survey is planned for 2012 and should provide a reliable basis for assessing changes in levels of food insecurity since the formation of the Government of National Unity in early 2009 and the partial economic recovery that has followed.[52]

ENDNOTES

1 D. Potts, "Internal Migration in Zimbabwe: The Impact of Livelihood Destruction in Urban and Rural Areas" In J. Crush and D. Tevera, eds., *Zimbabwe's Exodus: Crisis, Migration, Survival* (Cape Town and Ottawa: SAMP and IDRC, 2010), pp. 79-111.

2 D. Potts and C. Mutambirwa, "High-Density Housing in Harare: Commodification and Overcrowding" *Third World Planning Review* 13(1) (1991): 1-25; D. Tevera and S. Cumming, eds., *Harare: The Growth and Problems of the City* (Harare: University of Zimbabwe Publications, 1993); N. Kanji, "Gender, Poverty and Economic Adjustment in Harare, Zimbabwe" *Environment and Urbanization* 7(1) (1995): 37-56; D. Tevera and A. Chimhowu, "Urban Growth, Poverty and Backyard Shanties in Harare, Zimbabwe" *Geographical Journal of Zimbabwe* 29 (1998): 11-22; D. Potts, "Urban Unemployment and Migrants in Africa: Evidence from Harare 1985–1994" *Development and Change* 31(4) (2000): 879-910; J. Muzondidya, "From Buoyancy to Crisis, 1980-1997" In A. Mlambo and B. Raftopolous, eds., *Becoming Zimbabwe: A History from the Pre-Colonial Period to 2008* (Harare: Weaver Press, 2009).

3 H. Besada and N. Moyo, "Zimbabwe in Crisis: Mugabe's Policies and Failures" CIGI Working Paper No 38, Waterloo, 2008; M. Musemwa, "From 'Sunshine City' to a Landscape of Disaster: The Politics of Water, Sanitation and Disease in Harare, Zimbabwe, 1980–2009" *Journal of Developing Societies* 26(2) (2010): 165-206.

4 D. Potts, "'Restoring Order?' Operation Murambatsvina and the Urban Crisis in Zimbabwe" *Journal of Southern African Studies* 32 (2006): 273-91; M. Vambe, ed., *The Hidden Dimensions of Operation Murambatsvina* (Harare: Weaver Press, 2008).

5 M. Cohen and J. Garrett, "The Food Price Crisis and Urban Food (In)security" *Environment and Urbanization* 22(2) (2010): 467-82.

6 J. Hoddinott, "Shocks and Their Consequences Across and Within Households in Rural Zimbabwe" *Journal of Development Studies* 42(2) (2006): 301-21; S. Senefeld and K. Polsky, "Chronically Ill Households, Food Security, and Coping Strategies in Rural Households" In S. Gillespie, ed., *AIDS, Poverty and Hunger: Challenges and Responses* (Washington DC: IFPRI, 2006), pp. 129-40; B. Chiripanhura, "Poverty Traps and Livelihood Options in Rural Zimbabwe: Evidence from Three Districts" Working Paper 121, Brooks World Poverty Institute, University of Manchester, 2010; J. Mazzeo, "Cattle, Livelihoods, and Coping with Food

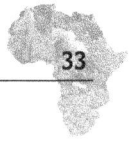

Insecurity in the Context of Drought and HIV/AIDS in Rural Zimbabwe"
Human Organization 70(4) (2011): 405-15; J. Mazzeo, "The Double Threat of
HIV/AIDS and Drought on Rural Household Food Security in Southeastern
Zimbabwe" *Annals of Anthropological Practice* 35(1) (2011): 167-86; M. Dekker and
B. Kinsey, "Coping with Zimbabwe's Economic Crisis: Small-Scale Farmers
and Livelihoods Under Stress" Working Paper No. 93, African Studies Centre,
Leiden, Netherlands, 2011.

7   D. Drakakis-Smith and P. Kivell, "Urban Food Distribution and Household
Consumption: A Study of Harare" In A. Findlay, R. Paddison and J. Dawson,
eds., *Retailing Environments in Developing Countries* (London: Routledge, 1990), pp.
169-84; D. Drakakis-Smith and D. Tevera, "Informal Food Retailing in Harare"
Occasional Paper No. 7, Department of Human and Economic Geography,
University of Gothenburg, Sweden 1993; D. Drakakis-Smith, "Food Systems
and the Poor in Harare Under Conditions of Structural Adjustment" *Geografiska
Annaler Series* B76(1) (1994): 3-20; N. Horn, *Cultivating Customers: Market Women
in Harare, Zimbabwe* (Boulder: Lynne Rienner, 1994); S. Leybourne and M.
Grant, "Bottlenecks in the Informal Food-Transportation Network of Harare,
Zimbabwe" In M. Koc, R. MacRae, L. Mougeot and J. Welsh, eds., *For Hunger-
Proof Cities: Sustainable Urban Food Systems* (Ottawa: IDRC, 1999), pp. 110-14.

8   B. Mbiba, "Institutional Responses to Uncontrolled Urban Cultivation in
Harare: Prohibitive or Accommodative?" *Environment and Urbanization* 6(1)
(1994): 188-202; D. Drakakis-Smith, T. Bowyer-Bower and D. Tevera, "Urban
Poverty and Urban Agriculture: An Overview of the Linkages in Harare" *Habitat
International* 19(2) (1995): 183–93; B. Mbiba, "Classification and Description of
Urban Agriculture in Harare" *Development Southern Africa* 12(1) (1995): 75-86; D.
Drakakis-Smith and D. Tevera, "Socioeconomic Context for the Householder
of Urban Agriculture in Harare, Zimbabwe" *Geographical Journal of Zimbabwe*
28 (1996): 25–38; G. Mudimu, "Urban Agricultural Activities and Women's
Strategies in Sustaining Family Livelihoods in Harare, Zimbabwe" *Singapore Journal
of Tropical Geography* 17(2) (1997): 179–94; D. Smith and H. Ajaegbu, "Urban
Agriculture in Harare: Socio-Economic Dimensions of a Survival Strategy" In D.
Grossman, L. van den Berg and H. Ajaegbu, eds., *Urban and Peri-Urban Agriculture
in Africa* (Aldershot: Ashgate, 1999); G. Mutangadura and E. Makuadze, "Urban
Vulnerability to Chronic Poverty and Income Shocks and Effectiveness of Current
Social Protection Mechanisms: The Case of Zimbabwe" Report for Ministry of
Public Service, Labour and Social Welfare and the World Bank, 1999; B. Mbiba,
"Urban Agriculture in Harare: Between Suspicion and Repression" In M. Bakker,
S. Dubbeling, U. Guendel, S. Koschella and H. de Zeeuw, eds., *Growing Cities,
Growing Food: Urban Agriculture on the Policy Agenda* (Feldafing: DSE, 2000), pp.
285–302.

9   See, for example, K. Bird and M. Prowse, "Vulnerability, Poverty and Coping
in Zimbabwe" Research Paper No. 41, Institute for Development Economic
Research, United Nations University, Helsinki, 2008; M. Brown and C.
Funk, "Early Warning of Food Security Crises in Urban Areas: The Case
of Harare, Zimbabwe, 2007" *Geotechnologies and the Environment* 2(2) (2010):
229-41; P. Gwatirisa and L. Manderson, " Food Insecurity and HIV/AIDS
in Low-income Households in Urban Zimbabwe" *Human Organization* 68(1)
(2009): 103–12; P. Toriro, "The Impact of the Economic Meltdown on Urban
Agriculture in Harare" *Urban Agriculture Magazine* 21(2010): 26-7; S. Bracking
and L. Sachikonye, "Migrant Remittances and Household Wellbeing in Urban

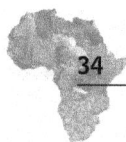

Zimbabwe" *International Migration* 48 (2010): 203-27; S. Kutiwa, E. Boon and D. Devuyst, "Urban Agriculture in Low Income Households of Harare: An Adaptive Response to Economic Crisis" *Journal of Human Ecology* 35(2010): 85-96; P. Moyo, "Land Reform in Zimbabwe and Urban Livelihoods Transformation" Working Paper 15, Livelihoods After Land Reform in Zimbabwe Project, University of Western Cape, 2010; T. Mukwedeya, "Zimbabwe's Saving Grace: The Role of Remittances in Household Livelihood Strategies in Glen Norah, Harare" *South African Review of Sociology* 42(1) (2011): 116-30; G. Tawodzera, "Vulnerability in Crisis: Urban Household Food Insecurity in Epworth, Harare, Zimbabwe" *Food Security* 3(4) (2011): 503-20.

10   J. Crush, B. Frayne and W. Pendleton, "The Crisis of Food Insecurity in Southern African Cities" *Journal of Hunger and Environmental Nutrition* (in press).

11   FEWS Net and the Consumer Council of Zimbabwe, "Harare Urban Vulnerability Assessment" Harare, July 2001.

12   The Food Poverty Line is calculated as the cost of a standard "basket" of purchased foodstuffs.

13   SADC FANR Vulnerability Assessment Committee and the Zimbabwe Vulnerability Assessment Committee, "Zimbabwe Urban Areas: Food Security and Vulnerability Assessment - September 2003" Urban Report No 1, Harare, February 2004.

14   Ibid., p. 14.

15   Zimbabwe National Vulnerability Assessment Committee, "November 2006 Urban Assessment Report" Urban Report No. 2, Harare.

16   Zimbabwe Vulnerability Assessment Committee (ZimVAC), "Urban Food Security Assessment: January 2009 National Report" Harare, 2009.

17   A. Swindale and P. Bilinsky, "Development of a Universally Applicable Household Food Insecurity Measurement Tool: Process, Current Status, and Outstanding Issues" *Journal of Nutrition* 136(5) (2006): 1449S-1452S; M. Faber, C. Schwabe and S. Drimie, "Dietary Diversity in Relation to Other Household Food Security Indicators" *International Journal of Food Safety, Nutrition and Public Health* 2(1) (2009): 1-15.

18   J. Coates, A. Swindale and P. Bilinsky, "Household Food Insecurity Access Scale (HFIAS) for Measurement of Food Access: Indicator Guide (Version 3)" Food and Nutrition Technical Assistance Project, Academy for Educational Development, Washington, D.C., 2007, p.18.

19   Ibid., pp. 21-2.

20   A. Swindale and P. Bilinsky, "Household Dietary Diversity Score (HDDS) for Measurement of Household Food Access: Indicator Guide (Version 2)" Food and Nutrition Technical Assistance Project, Academy for Educational Development, Washington, D.C., 2006.

21   P. Bilinsky and A. Swindale, "Months of Adequate Household Food Provisioning (MAHFP) for Measurement of Household Food Access: Indicator Guide" Food and Nutrition Technical Assistance Project, Academy for Educational Development, Washington, D.C., 2007.

22   ZimVAC, "Urban Livelihoods Assessment April 2011 Report" (Harare, 2011).

23   R. Dlodlo, P. Fujiwara, Z. Hwalima, S. Mungofa and A. Harries, "Adult Mortality in the Cities of Bulawayo and Harare, Zimbabwe: 1979-2008" *Journal of the International AIDS Society* 14, Supplement 1, S2.

24   O. Kuku, C. Gundersen and S. Garasky, "Differences in Food Insecurity Between Adults and Children in Zimbabwe" *Food Policy* 36(2) (2011): 311-17.

25   M. Luebker, "Employment, Unemployment and Informality in Zimbabwe: Concepts and Data for Coherent Policy Making" Issues Paper No. 32, ILO Sub-Regional Office for Southern Africa, Harare, 2008, p. 32.

26   A. Chimhowu, ed., "Moving Forward in Zimbabwe: Reducing Poverty and Promoting Productivity" Brooks World Poverty Institute, University of Manchester, 2009, p. 33.

27   "Zimbabwe Unemployment Soars to 94%" *AFP* 29 January 2009.

28   Luebker, "Employment, Unemployment and Informality in Zimbabwe" p. 29.

29   Chimhowu, "Moving Forward in Zimbabwe" p. 12.

30   L. Sachikonye, "The Impact of Operation Murambatsvina/Clean Up on the Working People in Zimbabwe" Report for the Labour and Economic Development Research Institute of Zimbabwe, Harare, 2006, p.27.

31   K. Manganga, "Street Vending in Post-Operation Murambatsvina Harare: The Case of Female Vendors at Machipisa, Highfield Township" Paper for the Living on the Margins Conference, Stellenbosch, 2007; M. Luebker, "Decent Work and Informal Employment: A Survey of Workers in Glen View, Harare" Issues Paper No. 33, ILO Sub-Regional Office for Southern Africa, Harare, 2008; J. Jones, "'Nothing is Straight in Zimbabwe': The Rise of the *Kukiya-kiya* Economy 2000–2008" *Journal of Southern African Studies* 36(2) (2010): 285-99; F. Musoni, "Operation Murambatsvina and the Politics of Street Vendors in Zimbabwe" *Journal of Southern African Studies* 36(2) (2010): 301-17.

32   At this time, the Zimbabwe dollar exchange rate was highly variable, not only on a daily, but sometimes on an hourly basis. In October 2008 when the survey was done, government workers (e.g. teachers) earned Z$729 000, which was equivalent to US$0.72 on the parallel market where foreign currency was sold (US$1: Z$1 000 000).

33   S. Mawowa, "Inside Zimbabwe's Roadside Currency Trade: The 'World Bank' of Bulawayo" *Journal of Southern African Studies* 37(1) (2011): 319-37.

34   R. Mattes, "The Material and Political Bases of Lived Poverty in Africa: Insights from the Afrobarometer" Working Paper No. 98, Cape Town, 2008.

35   A. Kone-Coulibaly, M. Tshimanga, G. Shambira, N. Gombe, A. Chadambuka, P. Chonzi and S Mungofa, "Risk Factors Associated with Cholera in Harare City, Zimbabwe, 2008" *East African Journal of Public Health* 7(4) (2010): 311-7; Musemwa, "From 'Sunshine City' to a Landscape of Disaster"; M. Fernández, P. Mason, H. Gray, A. Bauernfeind, J. Fesselet and P. Maes, "Descriptive Spatial Analysis of the Cholera Epidemic 2008–2009 in Harare, Zimbabwe: A Secondary Data Analysis" *Transactions of the Royal Society of Tropical Medicine and Hygiene* 105(1) (2011): 3-45.

36   Crush et al., "The Crisis of Food Insecurity in Southern African Cities."

37   Cohen and Garrett, "The Food Price Crisis and Urban Food (In)Security"; M. Ruel, J. Garrett, C. Hawkes and M. Cohen, "The Food, Fuel, and Financial Crises Affect the Urban and Rural Poor Disproportionately: A Review of the Evidence" *Journal of Nutrition* 140(1) (2010):S170-6.

38   J. Crush and B. Frayne, "Supermarket Expansion and the Informal Food Economy in Southern African Cities: Implications for Urban Food Security" *Journal of Southern African Studies* 37(4) (2011): 781-807.

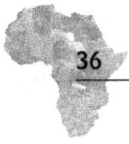

39   Jones, "'Nothing is Straight in Zimbabwe'."

40   See Endnote 8.

41   Toriro, "The Impact of the Economic Meltdown on Urban Agriculture in Harare."

42   ZimVAC, "Urban Food Security Assessment: January 2009."

43   Ibid.

44   Swindale and Bilinsky, "Development of a Universally Applicable Household Food Insecurity Measurement Tool."

45   ZimVAC, "Urban Food Security Assessment: January 2009" p. 4.

46   G. Tawodzera, "Vulnerability and Resilience in Crisis: Urban Household Food Insecurity in Harare, Zimbabwe" PhD Thesis, University of Cape Town, 2010; Tawodzera, "Vulnerability in Crisis: Urban Household Food Insecurity in Epworth, Harare, Zimbabwe."

47   Crush et al.; "The Crisis of Food Insecurity in Southern African Cities."

48   J. Crush, A. Hovorka and D. Tevera, "Food Security in Southern African Cities: The Place of Urban Agriculture" *Progress in Development Studies* 11(4) (2011): 285-305.

49   Kutiwa et al., "Urban Agriculture in Low Income Households of Harare."

50   D. Potts, *Circular Migration in Zimbabwe & Contemporary Sub-Saharan Africa* (Woodbridge: James Currey, 2010).

51   ZimVAC, "Urban Livelihoods Assessment April 2011" p. 47.

52   A. Chimhowu, J. Manjengwa and S. Feresu, *Moving Forward in Post-Crisis Zimbabwe, Reducing Poverty and Promoting Sustainable Growth* (Harare: IES, 2010).

www.ingramcontent.com/pod-product-compliance
Lightning Source LLC
Chambersburg PA
CBHW080135270326
41926CB00021B/4489